THIS WE
OF TH

JACOB SUNDERLIN

Distributed by Independent Publishers Group
Chicago

Saturnalia Books
105 Woodside Rd.
Ardmore, PA 19003
info@saturnaliabooks.com

ISBN: 978-1-947817-48-7 (print), 978-1-947817-49-4 (ebook)
Library of Congress Control Number: 2022940646

Cover and book design by Robin Vuchnich
Illustrations and cover art by Alex Cunningham

Distributed by:
Independent Publishing Group
814 N. Franklin St.
Chicago, IL 60610
800-888-4741

Thanks to the editors of the following magazines, where the poems in this book were first published, some in earlier versions or with different titles: *Bennington Review, Beloit Poetry Journal, Colorado Review, cream city review, COMP: an interdisciplinary review, Cutbank, Diode, EQ 3, Gulf Coast, The Gettysburg Review, The Journal, The Laurel Review, Mid-American Review, Narrative, The New Yorker, Ninth Letter, Ploughshares, Poet Lore,* and *Southern Indiana Review.* Thanks also to the NEA for featuring my work and mugshot on their website.

Thanks to Timothy Liu, Sarah Wetzel, Rebecca Lauren, Jake Bauer, and Henry Israeli at Saturnalia for choosing this book and their editorial insights in publishing it. Thanks to Robin Vuchnich and Alex Cunningham for making it look great.

Much love and thanks to Ed Pavlić, Marianne Boruch, Don Platt, Mary Leader, Karen Kovacik, David Trinidad and Julie Sumrall, writer-teachers who showed me what it meant to take poems—and myself—seriously. It was humbling to be however briefly in your presence to learn and listen. Thanks to Lindsey Alexander, Sandra Beasley, Mario Chard, Jaydn DeWald, Josh Diamond, Jessica Farquhar, Shamala Gallagher, Chris Kempf, James Morrow, Kim Strother, and Corey Van Landingham for reading parts of this book as I wrote it and talking to me about it. Thanks to the folks and friends at the Fine Arts Work Center in Provincetown, especially Jerome Greene, Janelle Iglesias, and Salvatore Scibona—it was there that I learned to be a writer as well as someone who wrote. Thanks to everyone at the Djerassi Residency and the National Endowment for the Arts, especially Katy Day, for the time and financial support they gave this book.

Thanks to everyone I've worked next to in kitchens, construction sites, music venues, digital "spaces," and classrooms, licensed or illegal, who are putting up with it. They can steal our time but that doesn't mean we have to sell it. Special thanks to Vertis Ballard, Ryan and Jake Puetz, and Matt Scherger for jump-starting many of these poems with conversation.

Thanks to my family—Julie, J, Ben and Sarah, grands, uncles, aunts, cousins, all—for always being there and for teaching me to read, by which I mean teaching me to listen. I love you all.

Loving kindness and endless respect to Rosalie and Marianne for our life together, which is better than I deserve.

Contents

POEM WRITTEN IN THE BLANK PAGES AT THE END OF CHRIS GILBERT'S *ACROSS THE MUTUAL LANDSCAPE,* or, A LISTENING

At the beginning of the war against the suburbs,
sitting with hard white buds
in my ears which I've pulled

& laid on the desk, starting something—Monk, I think,
maybe "Misterioso"— so quiet I cannot hear it,

watching instead the numbers my finger rolls up
to find a point exactly between
two places where the speakers are

& where I am. A place of
invisible borders. Or,
an invisible place. I wasn't sure which—

there had been this election,
this conviction. There had been a contest
I thought possible to avoid.

Sometimes my knuckles bled. Other times,
my head.

Put another way:
once I carried bricks for a living
which made it seem my life was a load of bricks

I'd been hired to throw through the window
of a bank lobby, again & again.

To get paid, I had to imagine
an upright clutch of white
snakes pushing coins into coin-sized slots

had hired me to clean up all this glass
with my teeth.

                    I have separated it
as neatly as I can into piles.

Imagine my face as a shape licked from American
Cheese wrap. A pile of saltines on a paper plate.
My eyes are two dollars in dimes.

Raised in a sack of bolts & screws, listening
to the given names of things

as if they were chewed: chicken wire, tire tube,
drywall screws in a robin's nest.
Roof nail, drywall, sheets of Pergo, drill-bit chest.

Brake pad, hacksaw, bleach in a bucket
& some bearings, greased.
Spot welder, table saw, apple-juice jug filled with antifreeze.

They said *a coiled mess of copper.*
They said *a buck skull full of rain.*

They said tomato start, timing gun, sledge for the Chevy
when the engine's seized. Live trap, blue tarp,
alligator clips & gasoline.

They said the Sawzall, the loppers,
that panel from the truck Ben rolled last year—

they said it, sometimes, limping
up to the bruised mouth
of some truck, a garter cut nearly in half with a shovel,

still riding, writhing between
two screwdrivers, held aloft, they said

listen. Living, moving, flathead to Philips,
sliding across emptiness the snake
could not see, which for a snake

means taste, means feeling with tongue
for what is not there & what is written out, slick & cursive.

FAMILY AS A WESTERN IN WHICH NO ONE TALKS

We had to take away our uncle's shotguns
but Big Kev, my cousin, is formerly a Midas
Muffler tech, unemployed,

& not discussing it. He guns
his rebuilt truck to say it: everything broken

gets fixed. You can feel there are good bones inside the shit
cosmetics, detouring down-canyon
where Crazy Horse

planned raids against Custer & where
Big Kev comes to boulder impossible

angles in a lifted Jeep. We're cousins, which means we're killing
an hour flat-backed, not talking, looking straight
up into North American sky, one cloud

like Randy Savage, the Macho Man,
dropping his big elbow on a sky

I can't say is like the sky Crazy Horse saw
since it's hazed with contrail
& carbon. He rode his horse fast

down each grade & walked it slow
up the next, Custer close behind,

I read somewhere. Their horses'
tongues dry as snakes.
Back in Kearney, I tried to listen

to Kev's kid out in the chicken-yard
gathering eggs in a Happy Meal

box. She already looks
through wire fence like she is looking
at a wolf through a rifle-sight

licking its paws in a bowl of dust, looking through it
into what she thinks

she knows. Some of the eggs she finds are
tucked in shit.
Some are full of blood.

JERICHO & SUGAR

It said Jericho on my checks
because the machine made us

deaf. *Man who lives alone*
needs a cat, Jericho,

Sugar said, whose knives
were always sharper, whose Ford

more jacked, a veteran
of many wives, the first

of two Iraqs, this the third
of his three jobs, third shift,

which made it holy, which meant
we could nip from the break bottle,

kick a grit. *You got to clean up the shit*
of something you love, Jericho.

Who decided who was what,
I'll never know. I could change

my name, turn my liver black.
But when break is over,

I'm on the pallet jack. Gary,
one eternity over, came to work

so drunk he *messed hisself*
& ate a tuna sandwich

wrapped in cellophane, Sugar said.
I won't describe it

but to tell you how Wonder
Bread crumbs fell on the pallet,

not snow on some mountain,
not the ashes of some burning city

we'll never see. He
offered half that sandwich to me.

CLAY PIGEONS

Some days he wore a bird nest
for a hat.

Some days my brother was so thin
he made the dead

jealous. We took guns
into a field & broke

what the trap let fly.
Winged things

so they burst into the bird
bones of some little

sunset underfoot. Lame, orange,
almost morning

colored. Fire lay down
in the smell of

our guns. Pop said, *shoot*
where it's going

not where it is & he said,
breathe. He ate

nothing but watermelon
that year, my brother,

shrunk into something
round as a bullet,

hard as an egg. Some days
I would hold him

down & let my spit
hang its broken yolk

above his mouth.
Sometimes I breathed

it back before it fell.
Some of the clay

we shot—fuckers,
not one bit a real bird—
before they found

where they were going.
Other times we just aimed

into the field
& closed our eyes. We put our hands

around the hand-
shaped parts.

TWO POLAROIDS WITH BLOOD IN THEM FOUND IN A JUNK DRAWER

1

The X my mother
pressed into each
mosquito welt

to show whose blood
was sweetest
was marked.

2

The paper towel
stuck to the gash in his forehead

[not a crown]

& behind, his work jumper, fallen from
the line & left laying

like a snake's peeled off part
pressed itself into the ground.

BLEACH

Back to burning tires, hot scratch of wire.
Back to gravel pit & grease spill.

Back to brass, back to callous, back to
nails in a paper sack. Back to the cold

solder kissed with a blowtorch so it drips
quick down the back of the fist

my mind is always making. Clorox will always
smell like the neck of the anointed

punk with the burning scalp. *Jesus is just
another daddy*, he says, stuffing forty dollars

of tinfoil into my pocket. *Nothing was never something
to do.* He means listen. Tattoo

into the hospital-white skin of the thigh
a grinning skull made with pen ink

& fork. He said, this is how you crucify
a love of ease. You nail it down

upon the hardest wood. This is how
you come to worship

each cut, every blue tarp thrown over a half-built car,
each bloody knuckle, the snail-shaped burn

on every palm, the empty-rattling jug of
bleach in the back of my brother's truck.

HOLDS

I loved the tree of woe,
the sunset flip. My brother
went through a serious cloverleaf

phase, could skin the cat, could Wichita
wheelbarrow like I never could.
If I didn't have a brother,

I would have gorilla-
pressed a pillow or given it the octopus
scissors which crippler crossfaced

could never chicken-wing me back.
Jake "The Snake" Roberts
carried a sack to the ring

with a yellow python named Damian inside
which he would dump onto his prone
opponents after DDT-ing them head-first

into the mat. Saturday mornings we watched
wrestlers asked a question
say *No more questions*

as if a war had come on
between squares in suits & these other mountains
of grease who wore neon tassels

& electric boots, who wore
the orange cowboy hats
of ridiculous kings & it was time

for me to pick a side.
The American wheelbarrow.
The armpit claw, the mandible claw

& sweat beat from the furniture
of my brother.
It was simple: to be the man

you beat the man.
You knew the man
because he had a belt, because his body

was terrible, broken as the years
are broken by the springs
which brought various flowers

& WrestleMania. Hold still,
we would say, kissing the other's ear:
give me your legs,

give me your neck, give me your back,
give me your mouth,
give me my name. Say it.

RED STATE

Appetite for Destruction was recorded here
in a pile of burning leaves. My cousin prayed it,

the hand grenade from the comment stream.
Now he hoards shotguns out in the shed.

For "Christ." I get it. Liking the imaginary
to be god-hurled. Walking out the piers of yourself

in a gas-can helmet, garden hose to breathe,
a bootleg pearl diver watching the bioluminescent

whatever-they-are of rage
hum up from the squid muck in your mind.

Diving in. On *Teen Mom*, all the beer
has blurry labels. It's been hard to hear

through all the stomas. There is a Coleman lantern
& a blanket & a boombox by the river

where I am saying this to you:
at work, why is it that men talk this *our-grandmothers-*

slept-with-brass-knuckles-so-immense-

they-could-never-lift-them-&-so-we-shook-them-with-alarm-

in-the-stillness-&-named-our-first-band-The-Vendettas
bullshit. It has never been easy for me

to tell who is lying. I once heard you say
the ghosts of steel & iron ore ships

are never coming home. You weren't lying?

TALKING TO SUGAR ABOUT WORK

Sugar has been fired by more chickenshits
in more kitchens, more chickenshits in hard hats
on jobsites, more chickenshits
with liquor licenses out of date, chickenshits with conceal
& carry permits, more
chickenshit bosses who wear digital watches
than I was. Why is it narcotic,
standing in the mud, in a field,
passing a joint & watching a hog
try to mount another hog
& talking about work? Sugar is making
ornamental refrigerator magnets
in a factory on flextime.
Sometimes he goes into the boss's garden
to pick her squash which he says she calls *sqwawush.*
There were these hogs, big
ones, scrubbing in a pen. *Which one is the old boss-hog*
Sugar wanted to know. The hog getting fucked
wouldn't be & wandered away.
Sugar coughed. *It's legal to smoke drugs*
if you're in a band, he said.

A MOMENT OF CLARITY & DARKNESS ARRIVED AT WHILE WASHING DISHES IN A RESTAURANT FOR 7.50 AN HOUR

The Wabash was never a river
& the river has never been a tongue
so why is each word a skinned fish
gut in the jaw's grass,
dressed clean in slick shade.
Cloudspit a fur-trader misheard
white water over white stones
Monsanto owns
like a system of drainage ditches
behind shutdown strip malls.
Kankeekee to Pallet Mountain,
dead sycamore through septic
fields from SIA to Oakdale
(*Best Catfish by a Dam Site*)
& at Frito Lay or Duracell
or Tyson it gathers grease & dead fish
like gobs of spit in a glass
me or Vertis will clean & since he's on break
it looks like this mess
is mine. So: when the river's name is Nothing
will Nothing still run?
Sooner or later, this shift is over,
our cigarettes lit so the cherry is held
against the factory dark.
When the river is called Nothing

will it still smell of sweat
that dripped from the keys
of the register of the last
open liquor store in America
which is a couch where a live trap yawns
on a broke-in body
wrapped in the elastic aprons
of the age, some Hoosier
disinclined to rage?
The river is blue-flame
pollen the aluminum plant blooms: arc, spark, sludge
flicked from a chain.
You can't be baptized in Nothing
but you can be wrung out.
In the floodlight
of a corn-syrup factory
you can drown. Cheers
to that & the rest of this *we*
in the back of the house.
The river is as cold as vodka
from the icebox, so cold
it tastes of nothing,
or it tastes of hot aluminum
& what nothing is
next.

HOW TO START

You should never start

a story I woke up
but I used to wake up
thinking some camera cared I was there

like a plumbob in the deep well
of my toothbrushing,
or a bellwether in my buttering

the toast. Then I went broke.
Took to smearing an invented yoga

across each Wednesday,
stumbling out of sleep.

I hung Hank Williams
in my kitchen like the religious will
above the candles
hang St. Whoever, hammer of witches,
eater of root soups.

Pouring out a whiskey
for the gods was an idea

I liked. That it knew, somehow,
to evaporate? That meant

they were drinking it,
all the dead-assed dead.
Which meant the dead were drinkers I could trust.

A STORY ABOUT A HOG SOME NEW GUY TOLD

The dude had *Born to Lose*
tattooed to his bicep
between stick-n-poke dice,
would rub our cached bowls
into his blonde dreads.
He talked & talked one night
over beers frothing like fracked
mountains of the hogs his family
raised, a thousand head,
their faces just one face repeating
a pattern. His inheritance.
The smell of it. You'd know them
he said by the numbers
in their ears alone, their faces
sick, pink, smudged pencil eraser.
Still, he remembered one.
The one. Who wandered up
the railway that ran
from Crawfordsville through
flood plain that has been flat
since the glacier ground
its way across whatever world
had come before. The hog
he said needed vision
to set a foot to either side

& loose himself from
endless track laid out before
any of us were born.
He said something about the hog
knowing what was home.
Instead the story hog
ran straight back
as the train slowed behind,
kicking up spark. I said that
he was new. I mean
he didn't know anything,
much less that mud is only mortar
& that work starts with light.
It comes up across
the truck bed of this
bleached out county, eye-gouge bright.
A lighter off aluminum foil.
It comes up because it is a weekday—
why else? We wake up
& make mud. Break the bag
over the mixer & scoop
nine shovels full
of sand & stand
where you can't breathe
the stone dust. Add water

from the mosquito barrel
& when it sticks to a trowel
without sliding stack
the Oldcastle 8 x 8 x 16
concrete block, a buck a piece,
36.5 pounds each, a metaphor
for nothing, ten bucks
an hour, sometimes I dreamed
all this before waking
to do it & if the mud I make
is good, the boss
will say, *Good mud.*
Benton County.
The known universe
goes north to Wooden Gun
& south to New Harmony
& when these walls
are finished, they will stand
until whatever world
comes next. It's anchored with rebar
we sank. The Portland cement
we poured into the seams
of vertical doubt & which ate
blood sores full of rock
into the palms my mother scoured

with steel wool. Leaning over
the sink, scrubbed bloody.
Finding new skin underneath.
I slept with my hands in clean socks
full of Vaseline. My mother
did that for me. If new dude
thought his story was about being
heat struck or sunblind,
no inside himself
to find, thinking the hog
he had made of himself
was what might howl
in finding his way
laid out, that's because
he was not the hog,
he was the train. He said he'd heard
the sound a train makes
his whole life. I'd heard it too.
Each morning we drove deep
into the blinking
stretch of that county,
before light. Each day we worked
among the bootleg diamonds
of anti-helicopter lights,
we saw the same sentinel eyes

of the new wind turbines,
blue as factory flame, the lame
ditch crosses for nobody.
We turned the same hammers
over in our hands
& hit the mortar mixer
to make it clean.

WORK, A SELECTED HISTORY

In a quarry, I was flow block, wet as spit
& white as the capitol we cleaved from it.

Your past is a hole, they said.
Thank you, I said.
That night a spider crouched

in the sleeve of a hand-me-down
I had worn until it went thin.
Its egg sac is empty

as the drawer they keep the oxycontin in.
The next morning I was a tendon
& I tore. Then I was a dog

who broke—licked the wet hand
of any man who spoke, who told me
I was more than a flattened coin

on the ruined fingers of the railroad,
more than a moss-covered bucket
of minnows gathered from a creek.

When I was a man, I learned to lie.
Soaked a carburetor in choke
cleaner, mixed mud for anyone

with a truck & a forehead burned
dark by daylight. Then I was mud.
I fixed what broke

& waited for the next thing to break.
Every evening, I gathered moss,
sitting, pouring something like milk

back & forth between urns.
Some days it seems there will be
no world not walled. I pour water

onto the mortar board
to make it thin, slap the mud
until it is soft as someone else's skin.

If the sun is a needle, I squint.

ELEGY FOR GETTING HIGH WITH PAUL

How buzzcut hairs picked from the cold bologna
on a paper plate moon smell. How your uncles

used to slap our scalps
& say, *Look at them skinheads*

sitting there / Don't they wish they had some hair
& other Army talk. How the Camel smoke

they blew cleaned the shears.
How you said *I'd rather eat catshit*

with a knitting needle than send a cop's kid to college
quoting Kirby, the only character

who doesn't paint his face
into the ghost version of his face

before robbing the armored car
in *Dead Presidents*, a movie we inhaled

too young to see the VC
castrate D'Ambrosio, shove it back

into his mouth. How *Shut the fuck up*
Skippy meant Paul

are you my brother? Under a jagged
metal caterpillar kids played on

we smoked whatever your cousin
neglected. Poured Kool-Aid from a jug

for the heatstroke dog
we found, shears of smoke

peeling the pink trees beneath our ribs.
Sat on a warm blue cooler growing mold in a field

of shit—like our lungs, giving up
their unmemorized thing.

ELEGY AS NOTICE THAT NOBODY'S HIRING

I don't remember his name, the enlisted dude
who said this town was bullshit as being

back at basic, anyway, stabbing
a cigarette through the plastic wrapped

around the pack, dragon blazed across
the psychedelic sky of fake-silk shirt,

waiting for the bus after work.
He stared deep into the dishwater like my brother

& I would stare at dead raccoons
floating facedown in Freeman Lake.

Said he'd bring us back a thousand bucks
of Afghan kush from overseas—*That's my college*—

saying he knows of a guy, just off base,
who could get this acid.

He said you take it in your eyes.

TALKING TO SUGAR ABOUT THE AFTERLIFE

God never clapped back
in any kind of lightning voice
or thunder-throated
& drunken slid across the sky
on bottleneck & knife,
or glissando'd down chemtrails
hung like a choke chain or guitar
strung above any neighborhood
I'd been to, but something
must have showed face
in the crust of the cold
blue-dark blossom of
saliva dried to the carpet
& *he wanted to be sky buried anyway,*
she said, *like they do in Tibet,*
so that's why she left him
in the hall after he OD'd
& threw open the windows
across 3rd St. from the bar
where we stood in afterwork
clouds of smoke
watching cops gather & stretch
yellow tape around what
we weren't supposed to see.

TALKING TO SUGAR AT LAST CALL

I had too much midnight milk
so I tested out the ways a jaw might

kiss a fist. Some days I just forget.
Two more & two more

& I'm full of honey from a rock.
When I leave—

I never leave. I just thread another page
off the book & stare

through the wobble of glass.
I can see myself there,

poling another rough pumpkin
through the straw

called intelligence like something a dog
dreamed in adjacent eternities.

A furry bubble full of—what?
A spitty button hole

the nothing of me works?
I say, that septum is,

after fourteen years, still pierced?
Prove it with a paperclip.

Tweak the cosmic marble
or something. Some days

I get this hovel idea. It's filled with pelts,
an old woodstove, clawfoot washtub

in a cabin built of
necessary trees. Making the most

of my hermitage, I fill buckets with the milk
of cheese-making goats

who have biblical names. Like Jacob.
I go into the cabin to keep terms

with the bewildered caul of being
thirteen, surrounded by the dead

who used to peek through the roof,
not so much stroking stringed things

& eating afterlife biscuits
as making sound like a wonky piano

dragging its broken leg
in a circle of Sundays. I could be that

throat sound a lame dog makes
in a shitty winter, something played through

an amplifier hung in the cold needles
of a silver pine tree, a song—

not just the sound of *yes-yes* bleeping
in the tweaking hour. Sounds made as if to say,

you got it right. These cloud bruise
songs are difficult.

But you can learn them, burning
your days off working

at little lung-clutched disasters.

SUGAR SAYS A HANGOVER IS THE AVATAR OF THE IMMORTAL SOUL

& calls his a Hank Williams which means
it's early, I guess, a cold can
in the morning, a foot dried of sweat
in the back of a truck, a motel
parking lot, a diner in some city
without trees, three days spent there
with empty bottles instead of hands,
a new record, the motel is breathing
with tape over its mouth, this rattle
of coughing & its worms of light,
this knuckle locked up like the gold
in a tambourine, this world which is
weightless, an hour of church bells, no church.

•

I feel like two pages torn from a closed book.
Thought I knew enough
to pick a watermelon for the dead,
white thump of it as it kissed the ground
but leaving as I left its rind out,
ants gathered this line
up my leg. I thought *bleach*.
I thought the ants might fury
a new constellation: a pale snake
crawling through a dry creek bed
who thought he could eat
everything, eat it clean.

LEANING IN, WEST 10th STREET

Say your neighbor is
just back from Iraq.
Walls so thin
you can hear him
through the night
punching door jams,
talking to no one.
A smell like burning tires
in the stairwell.
Some days he stands
out on his little porch,
casting a fishing rod
into the retention pond
behind your building,
drinking vodka
from a half-empty handle.
Next, furious
pushups in his underwear.
You can't remember
his name. You're up
at 5:00 these days,
pop a smoke
as you drive
to the north side,
past the burnt out

Frog Leg & Chicken
stand, past a wrecked
Holiness Church, up 10th
toward I-465 & past
the community
college that squats
like a spaceship.
You pull your hair back
with an American Flag
bandana, slide into
the restaurant
to open, spend the next hours
making burritos for people
you sometimes imagine
being drug from their houses
& into the street. I say *you*
sometimes, meaning *me*,
meaning, *you've already heard*
this one before?
My point is one morning
your car will freeze.
Won't start.
Neighbor—what's his name—
is out, getting into
his truck. Red-eyed, drunk
maybe, from the night before.
Know his name.

Wrench the frozen hood up
& hook the clamps
from the dead back
to the living so that it
unfreezes, so that the tape deck
will start up, left too loud,
as always, so that Charlie Christian
can slide down the neck
of the guitar, Lester Young
beside, "Pagin'
the Devil," 1939.
Leave the window
down a minute
as he looks in, rolling up
the cables around his elbow.
Let him lean in & listen
to something melt.

DELETED SCENE, 2005

That day we'd gotten so high behind the store,
a new language was invented

for the meat slicer, for the walk-in,
for the mop—*mangler,*

mangled, manglini. The CD changer
slipped from Eminem to Rage

against the Machine just as young cop
comes in, asks if I'm open & if I tell myself

they are just necks, cops, I can think
they are like me. So he is all neck.

Young cop is green as goose shit,
green as a pepper tree. So I tell

myself he's a kid, & when I say kid, I mean
my age. He wants to know if I'm open

as their squad car flashes blue & the blood
from a forehead brightens, then red

& the blood is black. *She hit me with the smooth,*
the bleeding man is saying

to his feet. He has no shoes. The cops' boots
make the sound of black mirrors,

the sound of broken glass.
Folded up in one of the booths,

moaning you can't hear what for glass
crunching, for cop. Hugging an iron, the woman is

watching for what comes.
The what? the older cop said, holding in his grin.

I can hear in this his wanting.
His wanting a slice to save for later.

The smooth, he says again, not looking up.
You know. You smooth the clothes with it.

He is ironing the air, bleeding from the head.
Think I'm closed, I say to the floor

& all at once he's not looking at
young cop, at old cop. He's looking at me

through the mouth-shaped hole
made of broken glass. I sweep it up.

Tip it into the trash. Later, leave so fast
I forget my sweatshirt hanging outside

the walk-in where I leave everything
as clean as it was this morning, as clean

as it will be every morning from now until
I quit. Walking to the bar,

there is nothing to stuff my fists in,
which are white, & raw with bleach.

INHERITANCE

I remember the 1957 Chevrolet Bel Air
is a two-door, hard-top, & it's primer-colored,
color of moss or mushrooms at the base
of a cutdown tree, like it has always been there,
rusting into dust next to the acetylene
& the cherry picker & the spit. I remember it was bought & sold.
I remember how much I've been told
a man needs a hobby & how for his,
my dad & uncle drove to Illinois to talk a man down
to five hundred from a thousand.
I remember sleeping in the backseat as they traded
this *brother-you-better-not-get-that-*
brokeass-ruster-just-gonna-sit-around-
the-yard-needing-fixed look, so he could give the guy his
buddy-throw-me-a-rope-so-I-can-climb-out-of-this-
hole-we've-dug-&-let-that-rope-be-made-of-money
look right back. I remember how often people say
you are from nowhere here, so that nowhere
grows inside you & since this two-tone Buick
has rusted inside the nowhere it rusted
inside of me, in its garage of nowhere,
among the flat caps of shelf mushrooms that grow
in the nowhere made of whatever this *we* is
made of—you might start to think of this as inheritance.
I don't remember buying it but having bought it,

riding back with my uncle, tailing the Chevy as it swerved
like a sailboat in the lane. I remember,
between Fithian & Oakwood, out 150, the light that late
fall light, the light off a beer top, flipping the dial
from static to static, I pushed the cigarette
lighter in just to see it burn. I remember a cloud
of dust, semitrailer in the other lane like a whale
we'd rowed up to, some dumbass
in a Mazda straddling two lanes & the wind
as it passes—I remember the cigarette lighter
popped out, red. I remember that car had a smell,
it's still in there somewhere, if you roll
the windows down, & sit in it—the smell of a silent interior,
the smell of something closed up so long,
never touched, which grew to fill the space it left.
I remember that day at the side of the road
he sat in it, my father, knuckles around the wheel,
laughing like he stole something.

DEBT

Somehow it all came down to a purchase
of metal for smelting & my father
needed to borrow $200
to give my brother.
Why don't I just give him the money
directly, I said & he said,
well that's going to
make him feel shitty,
& I said, well he's the one asking
so maybe he should
feel shitty & maybe
it will make me feel good
to lend the money.
It was a flimsy plastic switchblade
of a middle-class thing I was
licking the edge of
so he said, I'm not lending it,
I'm giving it, & I said—
& I had to, we were all the way
in this, whatever *this* was—
you weren't going to pay me
back then? He was quiet
for the minute it took
to let me feel like the scumbag I was
in grade school

when I quit smoking
white crayons & dove mouth-first
onto rolled maple leaves
& various other things
in green Doublemint wrappers,
a makeshift hardass
in a Reggie Miller jersey
who'd just busted two knuckles
fighting Jon Scott.
Jon, who lived with his grandad
& would be out of school
a whole year after a pit bull (not me)
chewed him up.
I kept picking the scab
so it scarred in the shape of
a snail. I used to think
controlling yourself was a matter of polarity
or of pull. When I laid brick,
I lugged the heaviest ones
first, cradled against
my chest, using the crook
of the elbow to fill the bicep
with blood until I learned to
just give up, exhausted, & dangle
the block, arms straight,

so the edges of the palm would
blister with long, wet-looking
white cracks. Still I moved
the heavier bricks first
so that the brain-numbed squirming
of late afternoon would come
with an increasing lightness.
Five o'clock approached
like oncoming traffic. Unreal.
On the first day of school,
I hid in a closet licking
a plastic apple. At the Guatemalan
plastic works where the plastic
fruit was made, respirators are
rented to the workers,
but not the thin filter pucks
they must buy & replace
at least weekly, although it's not hard
to guess how often a clogged filter
will go unpurchased. Melted plastic gives off
an invisible mist. Vinyl chloride.
I've never been to Central
America; I'm reading about it
on Twitter. After it's molded from real
fruit, the plastic fruit is hand-

painted, which is why
it looks so real. Plastic fruit gives
a model home a "lived-in
look" according to the ad copy on
the Amazon page that has
been search-engine-optimized
to come up as top-hit
when you search for "plastic fruit"
online. There are plastic grapes,
plastic oranges, plastic apples
& plastic kale. On the desk
where I write, there is a plastic pear.
I don't remember where it came from
but have packed it on so many
separate moves to so many different
apartments & it sits next to—
now—two broken antlers
& a jar of change. The stem is loose
& the pear is covered in dust.
Have I ever been tempted to
bite into this plastic pear?
No. But it looks beautifully
ripe there. One side is light green,
almost yellow, & the other is
a deep pink-red color

like pears never actually are.
It smells of nothing.
When you shake it, there is a rattle
as if there were something inside.
I used to think it was good
to move through the world
with nothing, accumulating nothing,
but this pear seems beyond contempt
somehow, so idiotic & shallow
an object that it should never be
thrown away. Looking at it now,
I feel many of the same feelings
that I feel looking at the cross-stitched
"Bless This Home" patterns
saved from cleaning out the ranch houses
of dead relatives. Lately I have found
myself collecting old army magazines—
Preventive Maintenance Monthly—
& science-fiction magazines
with beautiful anachronistic covers,
moon rovers more like Model-Ts
than real spacecraft, moon stations
like village glens. I place myself into the lie
of decorative mid-century
images, imagining how it felt

to read these images new
& imagine a future in which money
wouldn't exist but commercial
spacecraft would. These images
open themselves to me,
welcome me into their chambers,
a plate of fruit that is
lovely, ripe, unreal.

*

A few months ago, this poet
who went to Yale wrote,
When I'm sad I'm here under a Twitter
photograph of beautiful, gnarled,
older-than-our-imaginations
trees in what I'll use context clues
to assume is Palo Alto, Spanish
for tall trees, where the cheapest
one-bedroom costs $3,640 a month,
$1,500 more than I paid for
a semester of night college
in Indianapolis while I worked
two jobs, making breakfast burritos
& teaching the children of lawyers
how to write cover letters
for internships in Palo Alto,
so I messaged him, asking if
he would buy me a copy of
Swamp Thing #37 which sells for $200
on eBay, headquartered just down
the road in the Silicon Valley.
I lived in Oakland a while
working as a content creator,
a job godlike in its vague meaninglessness,
a job my bosses, Stanford grads,

called *eating the dog food*
or *dogfooding.* My life said,
For this pay, I'll eat your dogfood.
All day I copied content
from the Knowledge Box
into spreadsheets, moved my trackpad
to keep my Skype activity indicator
Green as I worked on poems
or read, then from 3-5pm
would feverishly write "How to
Build a Carport" or "How to Toilet Paper
a House" or "How to Dress Well
in Seventh Grade." It was
an honest relationship. It cost $20
a day to go to the office, to ride
two trains from Oakland
into the Silicon Valley, two hours
each way, guys with Google nametags,
eBay nametags, Facebook nametags
clipped to their belts.
Swamp Thing #37 is so expensive
because it is the first appearance of
John Constantine, English Occultist,
who spun off into his own popular series
in the late 1980s called *Hellblazer*.

Len Wein's original Swamp Thing was
the "muck-encrusted monstrosity"
who emerged after Dr. Alec Holland
was blown up in a mafia attack,
dragging his scorched body
into the swamp where it mixed with
the experimental plant-regenerative
chemical he was working on
in the lab, becoming a one-dimensional
eco-avenger who took part in one-off
stories & disappeared back into the mist.
But Alan Moore's Swamp Thing
is neither plant nor man.
After he burned up, Dr. Holland died
but didn't know that he had died.
His consciousness inhabited the green
plant matter at the bottom of the river
& the plant matter grew itself
a body—lungs, heart, eyes—
became a part of The Green.
Swamp Thing can root into The Green,
can disappear into the psychedelic
space behind each plant, each living thing,
can return to his plant body at will.
I'm no economist—money I understand

as an exchange for goods or services.
I am good for being able to remember
& compare. Right now, I'm washing dishes
for money. An hour washing dishes
is four hours of parking a car
in Athens, Georgia, an easy scale,
while two & a half hours of washing dishes
could buy me the most recent book
by the poet who went to Yale.
In two hours I'll wash 50-75 service plates
of various sizes which need to be
sprayed off before going into
the sanitizer, 10-12 sauté pans which
have to soak for at least 10 or 15 minutes
in a mixture of 100-degree water,
industrial dishwashing liquid
& Quat sanitizer, or Q-Solution,
before I scrape off the food
with a scour pad that tears the skin
off my palms, 3-5 cutting boards
covered in raw meat, salmon & chicken
mostly, & every couple of hours
I need to run the metal ramekins
which are full of salad dressings
& I need to run the silverware

through twice to make sure nobody
buying 38-dollar steak gets a dirty fork
& I need to run any of the prep dishes
the prep cooks use, as soon as possible—
12-gallon stock pots crusted
with grits, strainers clinging with pork
gravy, hotel pans someone
baked salmon in yesterday & left
in the walk-in. If I sound like a materialist,
it's because it takes two hours
& two trains & $20 to get from Oakland
to Palo Alto where the sad poet
is sad & I have two hours blocked out
today just to write this.
He never responds to my request
for Swamp Thing #37. I get anxious
that all I've actually done is
give material not for a poem,
which I would respect—he doesn't
write that kind of poem—but for
an anecdote to tell at a gathering
of writers. A more clever idea
would have been to post immediately
after he had posted & to have taken
a picture of myself washing dishes

at South Kitchen & Bar where
I was employed at the time
he took the picture, my hair pulled back
with the American flag bandana
I always wore, a pregnant & potentially
dumbass metaphor, my shirt
smeared with wedding salmon & grease
from the hotel pan in the dish pit
where I am when I am sad.
But I don't much like cleverness
or communicating with strangers
on the Internet. You say you're suspicious
of poets but really you have contempt
for them, a friend once told me.
Rosi tells me that I hold onto bitterness
because I like it. Of course it is
ridiculous to feel sadness
in the California trees, the Yale poet meant.
The world is full of wonder.
Which is to say he understands a thing
as his distance from it & what he says
he says to push it further away.
Whatever *it* is, it is the distance,
roughly, from his eye
on the ground to the top of
that tall California tree, which is power.

*

A few days after I'd fought with Jon,
dad pulled up to the bus stop
in the morning before school,
told me to get in the truck.
There was coffee spilled all over
the socks he kept in the cab, the socks
he would change into or out of
after work. On his way out to the plant,
he'd tried to pass a turning semi
on the left & mis-timed it, he said,
had to turn with it to avoid the wreck,
ended up straddling the median
on State Road 25, out toward Shadeland
where he worked. *I almost bought it*, he said.
We sat a while breathing the cold coffee
& the old socks, imagining his truck
was a little whale boat he had rowed
up to an 18-wheel Moby Dick
full of irons in its hide, white as highway
dirt. He said he was taking the day off.
There was a wild blankness in this.
Something I have heard, like rapture,
driving through McDonalds
for his favorite thing, McDonalds breakfast,
when he was supposed to be at work.

We picked through the white bones
of Styrofoam. We hit every AutoZone
in town. He said he was looking
for something specific & they didn't have it
so we'd go to another AutoZone
& he'd huff about how they
didn't have it & we'd drive around
some more, Tom Petty on the radio,
95.7 The Rocket. *You don't have to live*
like a refugee, he sang, tunelessly,
nodding along. *Makes you think,*
you know. AutoZone is an overwhelm
of smells, of grease & oil, but you go
straight for the book hanging by a chain
in the aisle like a dead fish, consult
your make & model & its corresponding
part number & aisle. AutoZone
was my mind. We drove past Wabash
National where you could get on
as a welder right after high school
& make 15 bucks an hour.
One of the welders had come
to career day at school to talk about
Desert Storm. He told a story
about the war that became,

in my mind, my life as a welder in some
possible future. He was so thirsty
that he hallucinated muddy puddles
of street water into Yoohoo, leaned in,
& drank what he imagined.

*

I have heard today that our capt
intends prolonging this voyage
16 months longer if that is the case
I hope he will be obliged to drive a Snail
through the Dismal swamp in dog dayes
with hard peas in his shoes
and suck a sponge for nourishment
he had ought to have the tooth ache
for amusement and a bawling child
to rock him to sleepe
is how Richard Boyenton
of the whaling ship Bengal
put it in 1834, but *Can't do it*
is how Puetz put it the summer of 2004
after I'd graduated high school
& he had dropped out. By noon,
we had drunk up a river
trickling from a cooler
with a mountain
we did not know the name of
on the side & lunch was always gray
meat, American cheese
off a Citgo station shelf
in the plastic diamond
we would later burn

with the empty mortar bags
that measured our day laying brick,
paid $200 a week under the table.
From a book on the back
of a woman's toilet,
I read how an ancient Egyptian
retired from plowing
& bought a stone sarcophagus
to fill with honey. Each day he bathed
in the honey, each day he died
a little more turning himself
into salve. I want to know
how long it took before he was breathing
his own lungs as they melted,
how long for his muscles to move
off in their sliding—and the eyes,
would they? He would know.
Would it be nothing at all
& for how long & that new
whatever it is, the honeyed one—
the part of me that could be sold
a jar of that honey
just now writing this wants to
pour it on the ground,
pour it down through

gravel to whatever is beneath,
whatever maggot, bone, whatever
kind of man. *Watch this,* said Puetz
& when they called his order,
he stepped up, said, *Give me a little extra*
honey mustard for the nuggets?
with a conspiracy in the form of
a question mark at the end of the sentence,
so the kid—baby-cheeked, zitty
as we were—stopped, glanced at the receipt
stapled to the top of the bag.
The *which*? & Puetz—*the Nuggets, man,*
Big Mac and a Chicken Select—
don't tell me they forgot it, he said.
His groan, his glancing sideways at the long line
that had formed at the register
while we were waiting, his bandana
crusted with mud, I repeated.
The face of the kid who glared
at the receipt, then looked up
the counter toward the doe-eyed
teenager they had running the register
too. Puetz followed his gaze.
That kid new or something?
Man, we gotta get back to work

in ten minutes—then, kicking me—
food's for the boss. The kid
with his order sighed, looked around.
Not a floor manager in sight.
He ambled off behind the steel tunnels
of sandwiches. Came back with a box
of chicken we never ordered or paid for
& nestled the 8 piece into Puetz's bag,
dropped three packets of honey mustard
on top, & Puetz wouldn't let
me cop a single one.

*

Mankind & the Undertaker fought
in the first of many "buried alive"
matches in Indianapolis
at Market Square Arena in late 1996
when I was 11 years old.
Because Undertaker's valet, Paul Bearer,
had betrayed the Undertaker during the Boiler
Room Brawl match at SummerSlam
that year, striking him with an urn
that contained the Undertaker's
mystical power—Mankind had
maintained the upper hand
on the Undertaker for the better part
of the year. The Undertaker was sad
& angry. When his eyes rolled back
in his head during backstage vignettes,
usually in some misty graveyard,
it lacked the verve of his usual promos.
This sadness & rage presumably
would culminate when one buried
the other alive, although from
the perspective of now, I know
that they would fight on & off
for the next two years, & the real end
of the feud would come when

the Undertaker threw Mankind
off the 16-foot-high Hell in a Cell
cage in June of 1998, crashing through
the Spanish announcer's table,
breaking several ribs, knocking out
some teeth & dislocating his jaw.
In October of 1996, one would bury
the other in a pile of dirt the World
Wrestling Federation had trucked in
from Indianapolis Mulch & Stone
Topsoil Delivery at $28.90
per cubic foot, a coffin full of dirt
for $200 so the Undertaker's hand
could burst from the grave, ending the show.
When a wrestler loses, it is called
doing the job, or *jobbing out.*
A jobber is a wrestler who always loses.
One day, laying brick, some Amish
with forearms the size of my neck
drank a sip of Diet Sprite &
told the mason I worked for his new hod carrier,
was *limp in the wrist.*
It was so rainy that day, I thought I might quit
but just kept working, carrying two bricks
at a time from the front yard to the back yard,

stacking them in clean piles, then mixing
batches of mortar in the mixer.
By the late afternoon, I was so tired,
& the grass was so slippery
from the steady drizzle, I slipped & fell
with a wheelbarrow full of freshly-
mixed mortar down an embankment,
spilling the mortar & landing
hard on my shoulder.
"How to Set a Broken Bone,"
"How to Mix Mortar,"
"How to Die Peacefully" were articles
I would one day be paid to write.
As I lay there, I thought I should think
there was something beautiful
in the way the drizzle fell
through the tall trees, because there was,
but mostly I was full of sadness & rage.
The Undertaker's hand bursting
through the dirt is the job.
One of the Amish saw me fall,
peered over the edge of the embankment
where I lay & nodded. Didn't say a word.
I stood, scooped the mortar & scraped
wet grass back into the wheel-barrow,
salvaging what I could. At the end
of the day, he said what a good mule I was.

*

I like a poem that starts, I remember.
I remember how my grandfather
sold camper trailers & drank himself
to death. I remember three or five
packs of forty-cent Chesterfields, a nipper
of bourbon in the morning
before work. I remember he drove a trailer
to California & came back,
found a dead carp on the porch
wrapped in newspaper. *Business.*
My father keeps butane in a drawer
& opens it & smells it to remember.
I remember smoking for a long time,
Camel Lites, but quit for good
when I turned 30 because I was
convinced I was dying of liver cancer,
multiple sclerosis, syphilis, hepatitis C,
Non-Hodgkin's lymphoma, various other
diseases that no doctor has been able
to verify. Half a pack a day + every day +
eleven years = 40,000 cigarettes.
One morning after drinking
too much after work in Palo Alto—
tall trees—I woke to a nagging pain
in my abdomen & ended up in the ER

after going to the urgent care
& telling them what was bothering me.
The woman had a European accent
I couldn't place—*yes, you need to*
go to ER immediately, she said—
which filled me with electrical panic.
I remember texting Rosi a screen-grab
of the GPS indicator that showed
her the hospital in Berkeley.
Where I am, I texted. I hadn't been
to a doctor in five years. I remember
a woman in the ER telling a cell phone
how much it burned each time she urinated.
The wait was so long she just left.
Four hours. They couldn't get my vein
when they put in an IV line, & when
they asked me to rate the pain
on a scale of 1-10 with accompanying
smiley faces, I said, *What you're doing*
to my arm hurts much worse.
I couldn't explain that it wasn't
the degree of pain as much as the consistency
of pain & the fear. When I tried to
say this, they looked at me
like I was a drunk child. The pain

in my abdomen is where I am
when I am sad. I remember being
wheeled up to have an ultrasound,
my ass hanging out of the garment
thing & the cold jelly she swiped
across my belly with a wand.
She showed me my kidney, my ribs.
She showed me my gall bladder.
Nothing insidious, said the doctor.
People who have the cancer my grandfather
had may sell you on a line of bullshit—
call it a fight, say cancer affects
everyone, rich & poor. Death, it has
no mercy in this land. I had blood
drawn five times in the next months,
learned the word phlebotomist, had a CT scan
of my abdomen & groin which one
doctor warned me was 200 times
the radiation of a chest x-ray
which itself is a certain number
of times the radiation of a trans-Atlantic flight.
When he said this, I told him
I hardly ever fly & he laughed.
That's not the point, he said.
I was sitting at Barnes & Noble

in the air-conditioning, reading a Batman comic
& drinking a coffee when the nurse
from the hospital called & said
there was nothing remarkable about
my internal organs. I got the first bill
in the mail sometime in May.
Being sad in the emergency room
cost almost $4,000, not including doctor fees
& the fee that the ultrasound technician
charged. At one point, one of the ER
nurses asked if I wanted an Ibuprofen,
& I said no & she encouraged me
to take something so I took two Ibuprofen
& I saw itemized that I was charged
$16 for medication. $4,000 was a full year
of my college education.
I had insurance with a monthly premium
of $200 dollars which I had been
paying for two years. Endless
telephone conversations followed
during which I accessed some previously
hidden from me person who was
capable of yelling at a stranger
on the telephone. One ER visit is
three-&-a-half-months' worth of

washing dishes full time. You can't
get a job washing dishes full time.
A full year of tuition at Yale
is 10,700 hours of washing dishes.
What the fuck do I pay for each month,
I yelled at an insurance agent,
crying. Every day in California
is beautiful & the same.

*

It cost $1,700 a month to live in Oakland
which is roughly what I made each month
"creating" "content." After the ER visit,
I bought a ticket to WrestleMania
which was in Sunnyvale, or
Silicon Valley. The names of places
are sometimes bought & sold.
The Undertaker turned 50
that year. My ticket was four rows from the top
of Levi's Stadium where I sat one Sunday
at the end of March for six hours.
Googling my symptoms to engage
the targeted advertising my panic
induced, I had convinced myself
I would be dead in three months.
Nothing is never something to do.
The Undertaker entered toward the end
of the show, still light outside.
This was senseless—when the Undertaker comes,
it should be to the sound of a gong
which kills the lights so that the Disney-
Halloween organ music may begin.
But in the Silicon Valley, it was just
7 pm on a Sunday in spring,
a perfect 70 degrees out, the sun

just setting behind the lip of the arena.
By the time the match was over,
the sun was down & the Undertaker
was gone. *Just working at the fair*
doesn't make you a carny—my friend Grosso
used to say that. Last week I got angry
at nothing—spooling monofilament
onto a spinner reel, I kept losing
the line, popping off
the reel, my grandfather's.
I was going to start fishing
so I could relax, but the monofilament
I got at Wal-Mart wouldn't cooperate,
so I stood up & ran full speed
into the kitchen door,
crashing my shoulder into it,
then I spit on the floor & backed up
& ran into the door again,
loosening it from the hinge,
took it in my hands & wrenched it
free, pulling both hinges
from the old soft wood of the house.
Screamed the word fuck until I lost
my voice, stood there puffing, the door
on the floor. I stomped on it once,

twice. Kicked it hard
with my left foot & I could feel
my middle toe break
immediately. Slowly the pain
came into my left elbow, shooting
down my forearm into my pinkie.
I was sweating. Later I called my friend
Mike to see if I could borrow
his drill & went to Lowe's
& spent 15 dollars, a little less
than two hours of washing dishes,
on a pack of shims, a caulking gun,
liquid nails, then walked to Mike's,
got the drill & the charger, cut the shims
to fit the space where the wood
had splintered on the door & fixed them
in place with caulk, then used a pair
of shoes to hold the door upright
while I drove the screws through
the shims & into the door
which still won't close all the way,
but it looks almost normal.
It's a week later & my left arm hurts
every time I rotate my wrist,
writing this. Today when Mick Foley,

who played Mankind, walks,
he walks with a limp
that began on a day he probably doesn't
even remember, sometime after
the Undertaker threw him off
the top of the cage
that night in Pittsburgh.
Good God almighty, that killed him,
screamed Jim Ross that night
on commentary, *as God is*
my witness, he is broken in half.

*

Before lunch, whatever bill
we had avoided came due.
Decided he might as well go in,
not kill a whole day over this—
whatever *this* was—during which
that dumbshit in T-25
would probably strip a pipe
fitting during the shutdown
or flood the release valves. I nodded as if
I knew. He parked by the gym.
What am I supposed to tell them,
I said. The radio static cut
in & out. He shut it off,
stared through the windshield.
We sat there for a long time.
In the poem, he is thinking how life is
this glassy thing happening
around him, between shifts.
In the poem, it is passing period, the halls
full. He is in his work suit,
the ironed-on patch of his name
on his chest. In the poem,
his hand has a dry white scab
on the knuckle which he sands
as he watches TV, his nails always

just a bit too long, eternally black
with blood blisters which he drills
into—that hand is on my shoulder
as we walk into the office
through the principal's heavy
metal door. He touches
the back of my neck so gently
I can hardly feel it, but I can
feel it. Warm—& yes, it is
rough. And he is shaking.

TALKING TO SUGAR ABOUT HOW SOME SEEDS WON'T GROW

They say each tree has a thing
you could miss—some flail—

how each pod leaks seed,
putting its shoulder

to a building's shadow,
how each burr and each bird

like a traffic chopper
sent through the ribs

of telephone wires
make the sky.

But there is no sky
to find inside. Untended

bile, battered angles,
I am a thing that thinks

a new tree puts out each nerve
without a word—some little

impossible-to-say plaque
that means *Tree*

is monument to seed.
Winter comes, a cold

can, the itchy blanket of
a hangover. Each tree

like a statue of a fist
carved from bone

so you can see the difference
between a finger

and a fist. So you can see
how this living's mostly

wasting time, half done—
some tree spreading its

gnarly knuckles around nothing.

BEST PRACTICES FOR SPEAKING WITH THE FATHER

First you have to weld one
from copper t-joints

& stab its finger into your chest.
Now stitch its ligaments

to the rotgut seats of a fishing boat
and set it there shirtless

on the Evinrude. You'll need to grease
its gears, so press your wrist

into a hacksaw—your blood
is his—& let it run a creek

down the arm, or slick back
your hair. Let each knuckle bust

write its new arc. This is
language. Draw a flat circle in a field

of corporate soy, then lie down
in a pile of warm gravel. This

is home. If his roof is rotted
to the rafters, help him to crawl

up a ladder with a tarp
over his head, a blue ghost

of himself. Hold the ladder,
so he can pull parts of himself

from himself to make patches.
So he can raise up the hammer

in the lightning. If he starts
telling you every hangover

is just a stump in a lawn, understand
he means every winter is

a legitimate winter. Thirty years
put into the 4:00 a.m. machine,

thirty years spent turning water
into benzodiazepine—understand

this makes him a monk
who already knows what happens

on *NCIS, NCIS:Los Angeles,*
Monday Night Raw. He knows

what happens before it happens.
The next shift, the next season,

the next thing that breaks.
He knows you've got him out there

on the roof, or in your little poem.
He knows as well as you the way down.

DUET, OR DEBT, WITH SUGAR

If some morning all that drunkenness was piled
in a yard like hailstones,

we would be given shovels.
The ice like eyes

that have been chewed
from teeth. There are no songs

if your tongue is not a trumpet
stripped of laws.

When the jaw at last is loose enough,
don't go silent. Don't slice off your ear

as an offering, or stop singing
out of spite, or act

as if a man were just a mason jar
used as an ashtray

that had waterglass ambitions. Sugar once asked
if I was a fisherman or a walleye.

Which I took to mean, had I been lured
from some crater, or had I clustered

in a canoe against an ordinary night,
leaning in close, imagining the bats

swooping between our heads
are ordinary bats?

That the moon is an ordinary moon
with the new moon in its jaws

& we're singing this duet
for gut strings & knife,

for scotch tape & rubber band,
for dead battery & flowerpot,

for plumbing wrench
& brand new nail, for wet mud

& mortar board, for dry paper
& dry tobacco leaf,

for your voice
& for this small streak

in a glass dumped of its light.
I'm saying, dead harp, sharp or flat—hell,

a broken harmonica
is hymn in Sugar's mouth.

He sounds like being born
in the gourd of a green canoe

at midnight. What comes from his lungs
like walleye rise from deep black water,

metal cans & mudfish
glinting in the muck.

Sugar plays, I paddle into something
we cannot see. I think there is

this world only.
Sugar says, *I think we're in the reeds.*

BLOWN THROUGH THE STOMA IN MY GRANDFATHER'S THROAT, THE SMOKE OF A CHESTERFIELD TOOK A VARIETY OF SHAPES

Not wrench. Crescent wrench,
left out in rain.
Not tooth. His crooked tooth, broken bottle cap

tooth. Not sawblade. The jig of
an unlocked jaw, crossbite,

not skin, the cut flap of skin
& the blood from my dead-
looking foot dangling in the lake.

A mouth as it says my name
from the bottom of a hole.

Not a jar. The jar of black eggs
in bar light, pickled, which he'd eaten—
gently, dainty, almost, like eyes
seen from inside out.

Not shirts. His shirts
which I wear now
in their shrunk-down size.

Not lies, twice-told lies—*This Bud is for the fish*
who lives in your chest, he'd say,
& each beer after that
is for his brother.

Not fish. Catfish
who swam from its hole
of shit & mud into a wet shimmering world
of shit & mud

while we'd wait on the pier—he called it noodling—,
stuck his foot into a catfish hole
& waited for what happens next
to happen. For all that

twitching, breathless, all that being nailed
to a plank of plywood,
flopping in wet salt,
peeling something from itself
so gently, like he was never even there.

TALKING TO SUGAR ABOUT GETTING SOBER

Lately I have felt like a fine mist of cells
rusting objects of their use: box fan matted

with my hair. Wrench. Knife. Guitar string.
Where I hold a thing, I worry it green

with salt. The old faucet was crusted up,
limed as a bell coral, so I pulled it & left it

on the stoop. This morning it's quick
with ants who move the world like ants.

They leave some trace, invisible,
to anything that's spoiled. Six years sober, Sugar

hid some bottles in the shed.
Every now and then, a jet cracks sharp white lines

against endless blue which he snaps
& keeps in his cell, calls them *chemtrails*.

Sugar says sobriety is like working a meat counter.
Which means, you can stand at the glass

& shape sausage into the face of a hog
thinking the teeth are never quite perfect,

but they're pink as crushed pills,
or you can ask, *Been here before?* & stretch on

surgery gloves & start looking for cuts
that could be new or might be

near to spoil, depending. On you.

NOTES FOR SOBRIETY

In the morning, eat nothing
& grits. Allow the wolf in the egg
called Wednesday the occasion to sit
angry at your table. You'll be nervous
to eat the berries he brings
with more complicated names
so pick up saw, harp, homemade banjo
& never play for anyone
whose middle name you know. Do it
yourself. Devote to it the day
entire. Given the jukebox, play Creedence.
Given the option, stay out of it.
What is it?—never make a punchline
of your family name. Even if you plumb
its gutter for crimes, then publish them
in serial, or trade paperback, even if
you trash the installments
under the most impenetrable of public
pseudonym, given the interview,
play dumb. Find real work
in a magnet factory, making birds.
Learn to airbrush & etch Crossroads
of America at the foot of the cardinal
in the crotch of the racetrack. Clutch

at this work like thick rope.
Start smoking, so you can learn
to sit, always baffled, always in boots.
You should get some good boots.

THE LATE SHOW

My father was neither the rope
tied to the neck
of the push mower he dragged down the street

nor the drag on it. He was the *now*
this in the Bud-Man hat my mother
watched. Neither was my mother the singer

who could coax into being
small fires—*When we've been here ten thousand years*
Bright shining as the sun—but at the toy factory

she slipped notes into dolls
as she worked: *Help*. From these draggings
came a gold ring & a rented suit.

I once thought they must have sat,
years, watching a television
that showed only still water,

waiting for something to break the stillness
in birth. To pass time, they'd tell the stories
their parents told, how my mother's father

stole watermelons, pissed
in the water bucket. How on delivery for Seyfert's,
such things as turn a man to Jesus

he saw. And when children came out of the woods
with bags of foraged mushrooms, my mother
said bless your heart

& stuffed them under the sink.
The Depression rhubarb withered, died.
Dug up from one corner of Indiana

& transplanted to another.
She felt that darkness full for what it was.
It was darkness. But it rode the tail

of a larger good riddance. The silver birch,
growing since who knows when,
burned in their firepit.

Its ash was unremarkable as stars.
The old ways are gone forever.
What of the new.

One night—this is years later—
they pulled paper glasses
from the back of a closet, the kind with a red lens

& blue lens. They told the story
of a creature they had coaxed
straight from the television.

The word for the creature in their telling this
is joy—the weight of which
I've drug behind me

all my life—some late show they couldn't recall
the title of. *Put the glasses on now*, a voice
commanded, & they did.

ABOUT THE AUTHOR

JACOB SUNDERLIN is the author of *This We in the Back of the House* (Saturnalia Books, 2022). His poems appear or are forthcoming in *Bennington Review, Gettysburg Review, Narrative, The New Yorker, Ploughshares,* and elsewhere. The recipient of support from the National Endowment for the Arts, The Fine Arts Work Center in Provincetown, and the Djerassi Resident Artists Program, he teaches at a public high school in Indiana.

This We in the Back of the House is printed in Adobe Garamond
www.saturnaliabooks.org